"*Water to Water* shows us the swirling double-helix, as it were, of the humane, a letter to the world in which two poets alternate in revealing, filling, and turning the universal in the personal. Deema K. Shehabi and Marilyn Hacker create a braided response not only to each other's verses in the renga form, but also to the histories that the subtle music of their words carries, making our humanity intelligible in a time confounded by manufactured reality. This book teaches us to listen for the monumental in the mundane—those intimate, irreplaceable minutiae of life that would define us, if not thrust under the rubble of war. In a world where the language of truth is asphyxiated, here is a return to breath and spirit, a work to treasure."

— Shadab Zeest Hashmi, author of *Ghazal Cosmopolitan*

"[A] stunning sequence of renga ... We celebrate these two voices, bleeding in and out of each other, quicksilver, mercurial, eloquent in song and silence, even as they celebrate the human spirit in a ruptured world."

— Mimi Khalvati

"This book's revolutionary form is most revolutionary of all in making serious political engagement and sophisticated poetic pleasure inseparable."

— Fiona Sampson, Professor of Poetry,
University of Roehampton

I0878687

WATER TO WATER

GAZA/RENGA

A collaboration in alternating renga

by Marilyn Hacker and Deema K. Shehabi

Interlink Books

An imprint of Interlink Publishing Group, Inc.
Northampton, Massachusetts

First published in 2025 by

INTERLINK BOOKS
An imprint of Interlink Publishing Group, Inc.
46 Crosby Street, Northampton, MA 01060
www.interlinkbooks.com

Excerpts have appeared in: *Kenyon Review*, Spring 2011; *New Letters*, Volume 75, No. 4, 2009; PEN America, No. 13, 2010; *Poetry Review* (London), 99.3, Autumn 2009; *Wasafiri*, Volume 26, No. 1, March 2011; in the book *Names* (W.W. Norton 2010); and in *PN Review*, under the title "Syria Renga" in 2013.

Library of Congress Cataloging-in-Publication Data available.
ISBN 978-1-62371-582-3

Publisher/Editor: Michel Moushabeck
Cover design: Harrison Williams
Book design and production: Pam Fontes-May
Proofreading: Greta Morgenstern & Rachel Teferet

Printed and bound in the United States of America

DIASPO/RENGA

M

Five, six—and righteous,
the child in green in Gaza
stands in her wrecked home,

grubby, indignant. Her hands
point; she explains what was done

bombed, burned. It all smells
like gas! We had to throw our clothes
away! The earrings my

father gave me... No martyr,
resistant. The burnt cradle...

D

breaks over the cold mountains
of North Carolina where a Cherokee
poet huddles in a cottage

by an indigo fire. She sees
the child and says,

This is the new Trail of Tears.
Calls out, Oh outspread Indian nation
Let's braid our hair

with the pulverized
gravel of Palestine.

Witness, she says, the unpinned
knuckles of this child. Feel
the burlap curtains whip across...

M

the third floor window
in Belleville, dyed blue-purple
like the hyacinth

on the windowsill. Nedjma
does math homework. Strike today;

but school tomorrow.
Coming back from the demo
they sang in the street—

Rêve Générale!—the slogan
makes her smile. Wan winter sun...

D

is grafted on the broken sink
that Maher uses for percussion.
He sings Frank Sinatra

in a deep cigarette voice
as the bombs catapult down

"It's now or never."
He pauses, and his niece releases
her breath over the scratchy

phone line between Gaza
and California. Where are the hills

M

...he saw from New York...
"*Marhabâ yâ Nafîsa*,
Girl, you watch your back!

Tanks and uniforms zap guys'
minds worse than testosterone

but you were gorgeous
reasoning as you dodged to
keep them from aiming

at the brothers behind you
dancing along the barbed wire."

M

...that your grandfather's
farm sat between, that you climbed,
a boy in summer

near the Syrian border
maybe twenty years ago?

You are still young. Our
hands touch over the open
books on the table

out of which you are teaching
your language to an old Jew.

D

The script leaps across
the page to smack
your lips, light burgundy

in the sun—
aleph, ba,...kha'a

this is the language
I breathe as love, you say,
settling into a cry

the first loss
is always

M

a word emerging
mid-throat, like the *ayn*, in an
emigrant winter,

a word that casts blue-white flame
across the café counter.

Nightfall. It's heady
as the red wine they're drinking
to hear each other's

stories in a third language,
the bridge on which they first met.

D

“What has changed for men
in this world,” she asks him,
as she wraps herself in black branches,

powdered leaves
sidewalks white as bone.

She thinks of her mother
entering her childhood bedroom
to straighten shoes, the lopsided shoes

“So that they don’t disturb the garlanded
angels around your bed,” her mother would say—

M

Her mother would say
"Blacks, Puerto Ricans, Arabs..."
and that was enough.

The front door slammed shut on the
puzzled face of affection.

All "we" were was what
was not the darker other
with his long lashes,

with her insistent questions.
Beyond the locked door, a song.

D

More like a barrel of prayers.
Soon, they launch into "*A'meen*",
their bodies perched on the *Kaa'ba*,

like glued-on locusts on smooth
stone. The girl says, "What sort of devotion

is this?" Her mother drinks zamzam's
brackish water and thinks
of another fountain in a deep

pine forest in Latkia, long ago,
the ocean sound in the trees.

M

The horse and the night
and the wide desert know me...
and this narrow street

where fine rain falls before dawn
and the child in the next room

coughing in her sleep,
window in November cracked
open, the Bic pen,

and the wind that slips in with
insistent chilly fingers.

D

In November, the Catholic woman
married to the Jewish man
sings, *Love the One You're With,*

her eyes gazing at the red bark
of the Sango Kaku tree. They were

each other's forbidden fruit. Now
they'll grab up some apple
pies from the Safeway isle

and celebrate another Thanksgiving
without their loved ones.

M

Her father will die
without seeing her again;
He's ninety-four now.

Safer in exile, they
plan insurrections in cafés.

She asks her husband
"But who'll take power after
your revolution?"

—thinks of the old man she loves,
the hills near Lattakié.

D

Thinking of the old man she loves
how trampled by sickness he's become
how he stubbornly smells like talc

when she smashes her face
into his ribcage.

She turns to the window
to watch another Cleveland snowstorm.
White ground, white blankets.

No man will ever love her
quite the same way.

M

Is it the same way
she'd thought of the young man she
ran off to marry

that she thinks of the woman
she meets at the library?

She didn't know then
exactly what she wanted,
but she wanted it

just as now desire wakes—if
it's desire—with its eyes blurred.

M

The Litani flows
under the Pont Sully,
past four Arabic bookshops.

(One is run by anarchists.)
She stops to watch a barge pass.

The Crusaders gave
her those blue-green eyes. Not that
interrogative

smile at the cadence of wind
tangling her kinky black hair.

D

Beneath the bougainvillea pot
and the jasmine-latticed balcony,
her brother looks back nervously

and sees the stray mongrel
cross the street in close pursuit.

He thinks to himself: I've
survived the tyranny of border guards
and one or two wars, but is this

the end—death by dog in an unknown
alleyway that smells of the sea?

M

Dogs on the port street
fighting over a fish head,
spoiled fruit—he can smell

the discarded orange peels
guards threw to exiled children.

He was sixteen then,
no dog, no child, a teacher.
Others learned to read

from the tea-stained grammar book
he'd grabbed up first when they fled.

D

On the morning of their first
departure, he looks back
from the car window

to imprint an eternal picture
of Jerusalem in his mind.

He sees his mother
holding up her palms
as he drops his breath

so no one can hear: until,
until we meet again.

M

The halal butcher
has a charity tin for
Enfants de Gaza.

I pay for my leg of lamb
and drop in all of the change,

walk away up the
rue de la Roquette humming
"Guantanamera".

On the Place Voltaire, a white
lady can enjoy the joke.

D

The joke's on us.
The white phosphorus
was first tried in Fallujah.

We are from Rawa,
a proud people from across

the river. You think
it's easy being a man
watching this thrashing unfold.

Sister, don't forget Iraq
and Palestine are one wound.

M

If this be a man...
don't mistranslate him into
a single language,

a single landscape of loss,
claim there's one story only.

He steeps black tea. She
boils water for cardamom
coffee. Would they have

words for each other's sorrow
if they had learned the same words?

D

He asks her as she turns away
"Do you carry the death
of a few tribes

on your shoulders?"
If they learned to find

their way back through
a field of turkey vultures
and pear trees, would she then

remember to compose a song
about water and moving moons?

M

Jamîl Buthaîna:
You still savor your youth, but
Age caught up with me.

The translator marks a word
in her *qamûs,* chews the pen.

Student from Nablus,
she promised herself not to
mention your dark eyes

but in this poem fourteen
centuries old, strokes your hair.

D

Who was that little girl with Damascene
eyes holding her father's hand
in the Shabandar Café early morning,

twenty years ago, on al-Mutanabbi
Street? Her eyes had excavated through him—

Was it his loud voice that angered her,
or his confidence among all the men?
Maybe she's an expensive cabaret

dancer now, and he'll finally find her
concealed in a bar, incense hovering.

M

In Damascus, she
reads her son's letter. He wants
to translate a book

a Jewish journalist wrote
with a Palestinian

prisoner of war,
from French into Arabic.
His carte de séjour

was renewed. As she folds up
the foolscap, she remembers

D

standing on the balcony
of her tiny apartment
in Kuwait overlooking the Gulf.

The smell of iodine so sharp
in her nostrils as she watched

the neighborhood kids
listening to Saber's crazy
stories of goat-hooved spirits

who linger at the fourth
ring road. *Dear God*, she sighs,

M

covering her face
with the abaya behind
the hired car's smoked glass.

Mosûl's main streets are jagged
with potholes. Before the war

she drove her own car
to the university.
She'd thrust the letter-

menace into her book bag.
Tomorrow at dawn she'll go

D

visit her father's
grave and read the *Fatiha*.
Who knows when she'll

return? The word *refugee* makes
her cringe. She'll go, but she'll carry

the sound of his voice calling her name.
How does one say farewell

to *Iraq, Iraq, Nothing But Iraq*?
She grabs a fistful of ground.

M

Her hands full of earth,
she kneels, in red suede high heels,
in her small garden.

She can hear the traffic hum
out toward the périphérique.

She's planting jasmine
after lunch, in a silk dress.
When she was young, though

the rich had gardens and books,
she made up the best stories.

D

After she died, he'd lie down
on the great white bed
where she used to comb

his eyebrows with her fingers
until he fell asleep. He'd wake

to the early evening
muezzin, the roasting *freekeh*,
and the poem:

Sitting in a garden
ropes of wisteria.

M

Sitting on damp grass,
she recites the *Fatiha*
on Dickinson's lawn.

Slowly, her Anglophone friend
repeats each verse after her.

"When I go home, I'll
either build a house or buy
a plot for a grave."

"*Insh'allah*, you'll build a house.
Keep that line for a poem."

D

Green house with large
veranda, orange-black
swirls on tulip tiles.

Fatima slices lemons,
dips them into salt, smiles

as the other women sing
"Tal'aa min beit âb'ouha".
In a few hours, she'll wax

her entire body. Lemon sores
on tongue, newborn baby skin.

M

A sore on his tongue,
the accent he has now in
his father's language—

again, a taxi driver
asked him "*Âîna darasta?*"

High-rise in Detroit,
hospital in South Beirut,
every cloned airport—

razed port town's morning-coffee
syllables he's never heard.

D

He takes the morning coffee
with him to the bathroom
where he's king for awhile.

The door locked, the window
cracked open—he hears

the gardener cursing
the shepherd—"You son of a dog."
He clears his throat, washes up,

as she stumbles in her long
nightgown, "*Sabâh el-fûll yâ âmar.*"

M

"Morning of roses,"
she wishes the greengrocer.
"Morning of light," he

answers. Early cherries ripen,
and the small sweet strawberries.

Last week she came home.
The sky seems wider, brighter
despite what's missing.

That stray cat is a brother,
the dawn rain a childhood friend.

D

A tangle of valley oak leaves
grates on the kitchen window
at dawn. She bumps

her right arm on the cabinet
handle and presses hard to ice

blot the bruise: she hasn't
heard her father's
voice in weeks. The purple-

veined flower on her phaleonopsis
buckles beneath her stare.

M

Beneath her stare, there
wasn't a thing to say. I
debrided her foot.

Outside the clinic tent, I
wear hijab and cargo shorts.

Sihem, who lost her
four children in the floods, cooks
for us all—and sings.

I sing. I've never been so
tired, or happy, yâ ûmmi.

D

Two girls crowd Kaplan hospital
with their insistent song, “Mawtini, Mawtini.”
This one is for Samer,

dying of hunger behind that door.
Freedom is always a song

smuggled through white walls.
Bahira and Adnan
sing softer now that the policewoman

shouts at them to leave.
They smile, clutching each other’s hands.

M

On Monkey Bridge, the
motorcycle leans, hot wind
puffs her saroual.

She clutches her daughter's hips.
The midwives' clinic is ten

miles up the hill road
in a village of errant
hens and flowered shrines,

where they'll help birth a boy child
smiling into warm water.

D

She looks out the window
and sees nothing but black.
Yâ ûmmi, it's night again,

and night thieves
conceal the moon.

Bed rest, and the forty
days hang around her

like punishment. The baby
shivers as she undresses him.

M

She undresses him
and she helps him undress her
as he walks away

and she, for a breath, watching,
embroiders a fantasy.

She is fifty-five.
He is her thesis student.
The only story

is the cadence that desire
gives to her long afternoon.

D

Noting the scallop-
shaped mouth of
the discarded bitten apple,

she bends down to bury
her desire in August's

tanned yellow hills.
She sprays the ants
with an expensive

orange spray and then
imagines their shrieks.

D

Warm July, droplets
of rain as she naps
beneath the silvery birch

in old Talloires, her feet
skimming the lake's surface.

She rises, shakes off leaves
from her hair, and watches
the Portuguese professor

eat a ham and cheese
sandwich on the monastery bench.

M

He breaks his fast by
eating a sandwich on
the monastery bench

since there's no one to feast with
and he hears his own music.

The book he's reading
Varieties of Exile
isn't about him

autodidact, polymath
in this foreign September.

D

He asks her how she
can tolerate the fireworks,
their celebratory nothingness

when this and that many children
have been killed in another part

of this same sky. He glares at her
as she feasts her eyes on the colors,
one variety of exile after another

on this high, parched hill
named after an extinct species.

M

An extinct species
bird-soaring thought, the twin doves
her father caressed

and freed above the rooftops
into a remembered song

cloudy with promise
of nourishing March rain.
The doves disappear

into memory, and there
too, they're an extinct species.

D

Her father turns around
to see her wriggle her palm
from beneath the yellow jacket

stinger. She sits fanned-out
on the lawn, the gruff

hooting from the fraternities
louder than birdsongs. He smiles
at her, handsome in a white shirt

and says, "You've come so far from home
habibti, but there's no shame in turning back."

M

Home, was it the town
where you learned to read? The book
open on your lap,

a book on the windowsill.
You looked at what kind of trees?

Letters on a slate
and in a quadrilled notebook,
verbs calling for nouns

or nominal sentences
of who, from where, you are.

M

Letters she won't send
she writes him in a language
not one that he reads

where neither the houses
nor the roads would welcome him.

Will he answer her
in something like a common
language? How describe

details of the dailiness
they'd both strain to imagine?

D

She pictures the tents
stretched out against the sky,
the babies born into cardboard,

the streets full of waiting children.
Does love survive in the camps?

He pumps up his chest, declares:
“There’s love in the camps.”
Writes the letter: *Dearest Hanifa,*

I threw your picture over the fence,
and out toward the ocean.

M

Her name on a leaf
of paper above the sea.
His name spray-painted

on a concrete wall. My name's
hesitant calligraphy

in a new notebook.
Their names linked by an echo
in an empty street.

The town's name where they were born.
Please write your name for me here.

D

The names of the villages razed
in 1948 stitched with golden thread
on a black tent in the *Made in Palestine*

exhibit in Houston. The names
of my uncle's daughters, each
dimpling and swelling with kisses:

Wafaa, Areej, Shaden, Loubna.
The naming and unnaming

we argued about in poems:
Darfur, Gaza, Isdoud, Yaffa.

M

Gaza, and Warsaw
where her father was martyred,
though that's not her word—

she weighs the two names as she
drives to the women's prison

on the Hudson. Shoes
off, belt off, full-body scan;
then, in the green room

political prisoners
open their dogeared readers.

D

She weighs the time on this cliff
under a low Pacific fog
where a small container holding

a man's ashes is being opened.
This one leaves behind a young boy and girl.

His father blots the
view from his mind. He sees instead
a bright winter afternoon

with his young son, years ago,
the wind rubbing the boy's hair.

M

Rubbing the boy's hair,
the immigrant mother stares
at water flowing

where there had been only sand,
has, is, an epiphany.

The other mother,
the sister who expelled her
from the home she knew,

if she wept for her or not,
disappears from her story.

D

Candles don't disappear
from the soft hands of three sisters
from Damascus

standing in vigil
by a large breezy fountain

in Walnut Creek.
The wind moves against
their veils, and they bloom

like an epiphany
against an evening sky.

M

With the *djellaba*
her friend brought her from the *souq*
Khan al-Khalili

over flannel pajamas
she watches the urban snow,

thinks about distance,
thinks, will there be more sorrow
leaving her foreign

city, comrades of exile,
than there was when she left home?

D

When she left home,
the early light was
the color of dark iron,

the open desert
on each side of the road

framed her father's face
on the long drive to the airport.
For every goodbye

between them, she sees the sorrow
in his eyes flame then snap shut.

M

The French poet and
the Egyptian novelist
walked on stage to read.

Twelve armed cops broke down the door
(unlocked). So Jerusalem's

Palestinian
literary festival
was displaced, to a

diplomat's garden. Nor was
this an Egyptian movie...

D

Many decades ago,
the Russian novelist said
to close the heart of a country

is to shut down its literature,
but the peasant still says:

let's cut this cloth
against the body of tyranny
and embroider our free symbols:

hoopoe, cypress,
anemones and zaytun.

M

Olives like pebbles
fell on the tarpaulin
spread under the trees.

We stood on ladders, plucking,
joking, were pelted with rain,

then sat by the fire
drinking arak, arguing
about resistance,

Akhmatova and Darwish
—olives to the press next day.

D

Darwish could no longer rise
from his bed to meet the beloved.
He was always longing

for that other city,
city of weeping guitars,

of *Gacelas* and wise lizards
who hold secrets of bitter roots
in their sewn-up mouths.

Sometimes, he could still hear the shots
that killed him, the gypsy poet of green rain—

M

"Come share my meal," said
the poet to the red wolf
in desert firelight.

Fangs glistened in the flames,
and a honed sword set aside.

The wolf was hungry,
accustomed to betrayals.
The man offered food

and a truce. What happened next,
neither wolf nor poet told.

D

The days were waterless,
and the nights engorged
with clouds—

the meal was a handful
of nuts, grapes, and dates,

like on the old caravans
to Mecca. He tired often
and slept restlessly

beneath the musk of her
hair: one half vanilla-clove,

M

A cinnamon clove,
a mollusk sheathing a pearl,
a wild strawberry,

humble hidden savory
engorged with a mother tongue,

not the origin
of the world, hell's mouth, flood-rift,
blind spot in the sea.

What are you talking about?
Irrelevant metaphors.

D

You spill the chai
on the rug at the Eid prayer.
The women pour in—dressed

in orange and turquoise saris.
Faint coconut oil on black hair.

This one is called Ayeshah,
and she calls you sister.
On the big screen, the imam says

"You'll reach hell's mouth
when you keep getting into debt."

M

He got into debt:
the boy's fees for private school,
after that, the girl's

but a goldsmith made a good
living... Journalist? Doctor?

His daughter watches
videos between blackouts,
afraid to go out.

No news from the boy since he
took that van toward the border.

D

Between blackouts,
he watches videos of
Grease, temporarily suspended

in Olivia Newton John's innocence
lost. Before *magreb*, he'd peek

out at the soldiers
from the living room curtains,
amazed at how these streets

where he used to fly down with his
dirt bike are now filled with tanks—

M

What grabbed at his gut
turning the corner under
polleny lindens

on a summer morning as
brightly dressed women headed

to market, what made
the broad street a dark staircase
(while sun tagged boys' bikes),

his impatience, vertigo
was, he recognized it, fear.

D

"You're the reason our cow
doesn't make milk!" the guard
said as he grabbed the boy

and dragged him off
his motorbike at dusk.

"If you touch me again,
it'll be the end of you."
He sped back toward his house,

the Western-style, red-tile roof plucking
the last rays of the sun.

M

This letter, witty,
flirtatious: six names for *horse*
from the Abbassids.

This one from elsewhere: they
shot a teacher in the street, left

the body to be
defiled. A border apart,
on her desk today.

She begs her not to despair.
Copies the six words for *horse*.

D

At the funeral, she
weeps at the despair in the eyes
of Leila's boys. She studies the photos:

a youthful Leila in New York
with black, shiny hair. Another one

taken at the mouth
of a Syrian holy cave known
for curing miracles,

her head covered with a stylish red cap,
the summer before she died.

M

A brown wool knit cap
pulled over her ponytail,
she read elegies

in translation. On the screen
Baghdad burned again, again.

Another teacher
in rose silk *shalwar qameez*
came up and hugged her;

they called each other sister
in their adopted language.

D

Sitting upright in a Tel Aviv
hospital bed, he composes
elegies to his departed mother:

The dawn nursed her face,
honey colored until the day—

He looks up to see Arwa
entering the room,
her hand on her cheek.

He smiles at her, "*Ahlan yakhti*,
Why is there sadness in your eyes?"

M

Oh moon, my sister
has shrapnel lodged in her skull.
She is nine years old.

They shot our father and our
small brother in the doorway.

Her name is Amal,
or Hope, she lay for three days
under the rubble.

When she cries out in her sleep
I do not think about peace.

D

She is afraid of war without end,
afraid as the crows
invade a school field

saturated with Roundup.
When she was a child,
she ate *moulokhiyeh* laced with DDT.

She thinks of her
boys growing up with Arabic names
in an empire liquefied by fear,

wants to weep, but prayers
amass on her tongue's doorway.

M

Was he shedding tears
of remorse, or longing for
that other city?

Cavafy might have written
transposing Byzantium.

"Go to the doctor,
yâ waladî, that looks like
conjunctivitis."

—keeping his hands to himself,
like the Alexandrian.

D

Put your gold bracelet away
she commanded,
or your twin in the otherworld

might find it, she said to the child,
hoping the Alexandrian couldn't

hear her. She turned her voice
to low and giggled.
"It's best to marry young so

you and your husband can grow
easily together."

M

Easy together
with her mother's brother's son
squabbling like siblings,

they're tourists with a purpose,
almost-flirt like near-strangers.

She blogs, bilingual.
He has been smuggling what she'd
better off not know.

Now, a bus to the border
where they will meet the others.

D

They will meet with the others,
and everything will change.
He will become obsessed

with producing strange scenes
with women on dying trees
in his movies.

She'll no longer
let slip his attraction for the
other actors,

preferring instead to fight
it out, no more denial.

M

Cloud cuneiforms,
the calligraphy of rain,
alphabets of sand

slip through her fingers as the
old woman copies the words

of a couplet by
Abu al-'Atahiyya
"*Death is certain yet*

I am still joyful, as if
I knew death through denial."

D

Clothes strung up on
the crepe myrtle blossoms,
they sneak into the hammock

to make love in a warm drizzle,
hoping it's dark enough so

that the old woman couldn't see
them, their denial of what they've
uprooted on hold for a moment

as the wetness hangs
onto their skin, ever-porous.

M

"The revolution
will be televised!" Ashraf
tweets from Tahrîr Square.

Mourad gets his grandmother
on the phone, near the window

she opens to look
down at the street, "A moving
carpet of people!

yâ habîbî I'm going
out, and bringing them water."

D

A grandmother, a physician,
tells the reporter
with a glint in her eyes, “I’m 80 years,

but I’m ready to fight.”
Her words pierce the hearts

of peacelovers strolling
the sidewalks of an affluent
suburb deep in America.

In one long breath, she recounts
the history, as news of torture
foams over cyber waves.

M

"Now they all know one
word of Arabic: Tahrîr
means liberation!"

"They may know a few others
before the week is out."

"Maybe '*ath-thaura,*'
and why not the resistance
al-muqâwama!"

"By the end of the week they'll
hear from *al-mukhabarât*..."

D

By the end of the week,
Google executives
will keep writing the *mukhabarât*

"What happened to Wael,
taken away in broad daylight?"

She prays for him quietly,
as she reads Dalia's blog
about dragonflies floating

above the fingertips
of protestors in Tahrîr Square.

M

Chams calls his mother,
and she talks to him in code:
"It rained yesterday,

a strong cold wind from the mountains
blew down the telephone lines.

Now the power's back."
A YouTube of the demo
on his Apple screen,

but not his younger brother's
face in the tide of faces.

D

The fire blew across
those Paris Gardens
in Gaza by the sea,

the same gardens he'd replant
each time they were scorched,

this time by unknowns.
No tide came to sweep
the ashen lemons away.

Only words in a newspaper
"Cowardly assailants: don't return."

M

Returning at last
she requested a visa
as she'd done before.

The man at the embassy
asked, "Are you a journalist?"

Not exactly truth
to declare that she wasn't
—who knew what she'd write?—

but she said, "No." Nonetheless
she didn't get the visa.

D

He forced his eyes away,
as he'd done before,
when she entered the darkening

study just before *if'tar*,
her lemon-verbena skin

scent bursting in the air.
Then, she'd place her arms,
around his neck, but all he could

think of was another mother
in another land, a limp child in her arms.

M

He is becoming
an American poet
in his ellipses

lacunae and retentions,
deceptively simple words,

but song and structure
of his first language linger,
those root-keys that can

fold, blossom into wild but
logical alternatives.

D

Small but sharp thirsts
in the ellipses of no water,
the mind quieting

on the hidden birth
in the partridge nest

outside the window.
She looks for the runt
of the pack

while the cumin seeds
sizzle in the pan.

M

In a Damascene
pizza parlor they worked on
translations of Plath,

stacking up saucers of sweet
thick coffee they drank till dusk.

Two years later, one
portable phone's been cut off;
no number to call.

The now-distant friend translates
silence that's not poetry.

D

A year later, she decides
to join him in Ramallah—
her research on Palestinian

youth on the desk next to the jasmine.
Sometimes, she stands with him

at the checkpoints,
takes his hand, pins it
into hers, counts

how many metal doors
it takes to get to the other side.

M

The eggplant curry
she made for herself eaten,
she washes the dishes,

turns out the kitchen light and
watches the quieting street.

Is she like Li Po
with her third, last glass of wine,
the midnight window,

the high nailclipping moon and
the plants that got through winter?

D

A whispered confession
about a red bead necklace
she stole when she was seven,

and newspapers columnists
warn of the coming Depression.

Is she so preoccupied with
what's ahead that she forgets
the hum of cicadas outside

the midnight window, the muffled sound
of the BART train speeding by?

M

The night bus speeds by
without her flagging it down
from the bus-stop bench.

She lights one more cigarette
and looks up at two windows

alight in pocked walls,
where damasked shadows gesture
behind the curtains

under a moon that sums up
what she knows about distance.

D

The sun's amber knows how to light
the salix from within,
measures the distance

between the first appearance of Um Kul-
thum reciting *Qur'an* in an angelic voice

and her bleeding *ma'waal.*
She comes upon the hushed stage,
heavy in winter velvet and sings

"What I saw before my eyes saw
you was a wasted life."

M

I slept in Yarmouk
and I dreamed of Palestine.
When I'm asleep here

I dream I'm sleeping in the
camp, dreaming of Palestine

but when they're bombing
Syrian cities, killing
Syrian children,

saying it's for Palestine,
I don't want that Palestine.

M

"My father was shocked
to have his cheek kissed by
a woman he'd just met,"

said my friend. I was ashamed
I'd done something unseemly.

"At home, we're always
touching and kissing, cousins, friends,
people we've just met,"

said the doctor from Cairo,
and grinned as she squeezed my hand.

D

Nadia grinned and said
"No offense to the Aunties,
but putting us out here in the shack

without asking us was a
bad idea." The girls

nodded in agreement
as the thick fog
stiffened outside our window.

We turned to the helping
verbs, the scent of chicken feathers in the air—

M

When the worst recedes,
the night soldiers' wreckage,
the boy with the knife,

there are verbs to conjugate,
grammar books' bland sentences

in which a young man
gets off a train, a schoolgirl
runs to catch a bus,

the ruptured world composes
yumkininî ân. I might.

D

From his school window, he sees
sparrows dive into watermelon seeds,
but he's still so frightened

of the man from the settlement
who loiters in front of his school

just to rupture his world.
It's our soul they seek
to destroy, he overheard

his father say long ago
before he was taken to prison.

M

“My body is mine,
and it’s nobody’s honor,”
she wrote on her chest,

then the name of her group that
she spray-painted on a wall.

She’s been in prison
for two months this week, she’ll be
tried, “desecration,

consorting with criminals...”
whose was that revolution?

D

Whose interpretation of the holy text,
she demands to know, is the right
one? Ayeshah rode into battles,

her place definitely
in and out of the home.

"Ours is not a caravan
of despair," said the learned
sheikh with tears, quoting Rumi.

She folds her arms into her chest.
I am done with narrowness.

M

She stands in line with
other asylum seekers
in fall rain outside

the Préfécture de Police
for her resident's permit.

After two hours, is
scanned, seated, to wait some more.
She'd like to declare

"'*Sajjil, âna 'arabî*'"
the day before Yom Kippur.

D

After ten years, she stands
on an October afternoon
waiting at the Rafah border

to catch a glimpse
of her son, her firstborn,

to touch his hand.
"Better for him to be in Gaza
than a prison in Israel."

She wraps an embroidered shawl
around her shoulders and waits.

GAZA/RENGA

M

No, it's not theater—
men in a cage, forbidden
to stand, sit, lie down.

Perpetually kneeling.
Clandestine, one stretches

his arms, lowers his
head: position of prayer.
A photo smuggled

out, online. Theater
of cruelty? No, it's real.

D

Real as hunger pangs;
the milk drying in her breasts
as the baby hangs

so limp in her thin, bronzed arms.
She shouts at the camera:

"Devils are less cruel
than this army of cowards.
Only God doesn't

fade in his pouring mercy."
Her eyes are deep olive brown.

M

Zeit zeitoun on a
plate; tear a piece of warm bread,
dip it in while you

listen to your friends argue
(Syrian and Lebanese).

Tear more bread for the
baba ghanoush; don't mention
Gaza, because she

has a cousin waiting to
get out; his brother's staying.

D

She stays because where
else is there to flee? London
flat sold two decades

ago after the first war.
Every city bleeds a new

exile, every street
is an unfinished half-love.
Her memory rests

on a clear-cut belonging:
her hand, his chest, sun dimming.

M

The phone in her hand
has abruptly gone silent.
A moment ago

her cousin was describing
how his two sons recited

what they'd learned at school,
even though "school" was only
a teacher, a tent,

children sitting in the dust,
pens poised. Then the phone went dead.

D

Silence of teachers
in white America,
silence of bankers,

of pastors and professors,
who go home and tuck their own

children into bed—
no thought of Arwa, Basil,
Mohammed, Kayes, Baz.

Silence of friends who tire
of your grief, of genocide.

M

I'm worn out with grief—
not yours, ya azizti, mine.
It gnaws at my heart.

An impervious heatwave
empties the streets. July sky

deceptively blue.
Outside, it's too hot to breathe.
Names known and unknown

in a WhatsApp, in the news.
Can he/she/ each one be saved?

D

An empty jetty
beckons in this calm beach town
as you bring a shell

to your ear & hear the loose
moans of the ocean. If you

wait long enough, you'll
know what suffering is.
A mother buries

her child in the house's walls
while tanks roam in Gaza's streets.

M

Her eyes roam the school-
yard from the shady corner
where she sits. She's four,

and she'd just been watching her
big brother playing football

with their cousin. Then
an explosion, out of a
tale of jinns, but it's

no fable, dust in her eyes.
She runs, shouts her brother's name.

D

A jinn looks over
her sleeping body as she
wakes from a dream

where she sees her father perched
on a green terraced hillside —

O' big distances,
how many sorrows are veiled
when daughterhood dies?

She gets up, washes her face,
greets her son: good morning love.

M

This morning the streets
are too hot to walk as far
as the market square

deserted now anyway.
Only a yellow stray dog

sniffs empty wooden
crates. I walked here anyway,
just to be outdoors.

No squash, aubergines, merchants,
women with caddies, choosing.

D

Choosing to defy
all war criminals, the lone
Palestinian,

Rashida Tlaib, steadfast in
her gaze in the Congress hall.

In her eyes: the land's
anemones, olive trees—
You go girl, your veins

are Palestinian, your smile,
from the river to sea.

M

A river runs through
Paris, where I lived twelve years.
Two hold Manhattan

between them. The Litani
rises near Baalbek, flows to

the sea near Sidon,
mired with industrial waste.
The Jordan ends

in salt water, sand and songs.
Now it's a river of tears.

D

The shimmer runs long
on the Bosphorus, reminds
her of Lake Lehman.

Summer rain blurs the news—
torture camps; a boy makes his bed

between his two dead
parents. She curses all wars
under her breath, questions

the Black Sea. In the Sufi
mosque, a whirl weaves sky and earth.

M

Leaden August sky
in Manhattan. Everything
aches. Humidity;

announced assassinations.
Kill the negotiators?

They do. Once I sat
against the wall of the Blue
Mosque, with an Afghan

exile, heads bowed. She whispered
the prayers, while I listened.

D

Under the white oak,
she bows her head, copper streaks
in her hair. The breeze

is an ember. She counts five
slain children on the floor. No

mother, no father
to pray over them. Half-words
from well-meaning friends.

Only Faiz's poem calms:
Where is the road to your lights?

M

The lights go on in
five hundred apartments I
see from my window.

Dusk of a late summer day.
Home is an ocean away.

Most of my friends are
refugees and exiles, at
home in some new home,

with some new language to say
Independence! حرية!

D

No home but the one,
where dragonflies pond-simmer,
where the body moves

as an auxiliary
to other bodies, where plums

rot & uncles,
aunts, little bandits fade in,
sing to what was once

a blushing sea, an orchard,
a long, verdurous kiss.

M

“I die each long day.
The cell is like a closed box
that no air enters.

There is only a toilet,
above it, a barred window,

which they later closed.
The slits in the door, closed too.
I suffocate and

wait for the hours to pass, breathe
what I can to stay alive.”

(Khalida Jarrar, political prisoner)

D

The land here gestures
toward the sky—no fence in sight.
From slits in the door,

we see trees falling with no
witnesses in the forest—

When our cities go
down in front of our eyes,
we clutch each other's

faces, remembering our
promises to the tether.

M

Live on promises
of okra in the market,
maybe aubergines!

A classroom with a teacher
writing words on the blackboard,

outside the window,
a blue sky no bombers cross.
You imagine your

big sister telling you of
her college in Ramallah…

but she's in the next
room, bored, with her telephone
and the notebooks she

has been filling with ennui
and terror, alternating.

D

She imagines birds
catching the first light, their bronze
tails swooping away

her sorrow, borrowed from her
grandmother, who did not get

it from hers. She thinks
of her ancestors, passing
like Pismo Beach clouds.

Strangers make room for her when
she walks on the sand, sensing.

They call it inter-
generational. She shrugs
and hums Fairuz, voice

velvet-soaring: visit me
once a year lest you forget.

M

Sometimes I forget
the screen of privilege, its
aleatoric

distancing famine and war
because of geography.

That girl, sitting on
the ground between two tents, writes
in her notebook. Carts

and people pass by (sewage
too). She thinks of the next word.

D

"Palestinians,"
wrote Taha Abderrahmane
"live on a cosmic

plane." How many words for veiled
suffering can the Sufis

hide in a garden
in a Berkeley café where
blooming bees dive

into penstemon blossoms
on a cold autumn morning?

M

« Autumn in New York… »
I think of effervescent
autumn in Beirut,

four years ago when I had
a work permit and a job.

The steep road down to
the sea. Trilingual bookshops.
Old men debating

politics, too involved to
ring up the novel I'd found.

Cars, jammed in every
direction, flee exploding
pagers, then buildings.

No one is safe. No one is
safe. No one ever is safe.

D

Mornings in the field
under the steep, jagged hill,
she feels a little

safe. Lindens and plum trees laugh
as the wind sweeps them.

She vows to make this
a memory: her body
resting on a bark, lilac

scent from the grassy area
where her husband gathers leaves

to make a wreath. Kids
play frisbee. Is this a Pax
Americana?

On the sky's open canvas,
sharp-shinned hawks fly overhead.

M

Buzzing overhead
malevolently, warplanes
frequent the market,

drown out the merchants vaunting
tomatoes, pomegranates

(it's the season). In
Hamra, life's almost normal
(Katia wrote to me

yesterday). The hospital,
though, receives people wounded

in ways the doctors
never saw before, even
the ones old enough

to have worked in the last war.
The road to the airport is closed.

D

What closes the heart
is the live-streamed genocide.
Tanya Haj Hassan

says, “Can you imagine throngs
of missing children, can you?”

Her kilned eyes tarry
on the viewer. Some clueless
anchorwoman is stripped.

I follow the sunset, head
west. They march the men and boys

to ______. The artist
is killed, the boy is burning
alive while attached

to an IV. O God: where’s
your infinite mercy, where?

M

Where are the Just, now?
"Where is Abu Fadi?" wrote
June Jordan, was it

forty years ago? It was.
She died young, and nothing changed.

A son, a husband,
stripped to their briefs, marched away
with Israeli guns

fixed on them. Where is Marwan,
Hadi? Who'll live to witness?

D

Wafaa' said bury me
in a shroud so I can breathe.
Witness the flesh speak,

said the scholar at Berkeley,
breathlessly. What is sacred

now? How do we love?
How do we bring the whole back?
The questions haunt them

as they step out at sunset
the air crisp, the heart closing.

MARILYN HACKER is an American poet, translator, and critic. She is Professor of English emerita at the City College of New York. She is the author of nineteen books of poems, most recently *Calligraphies* (Norton, 2023), and another collaboration, *A Different Distance*, written with Karthika Naïr (Milkweed Editions, 2021). *Presentation Piece* won the National Book Award and in 2010, she received the PEN/Voelcker Award for Poetry. Her translations include Samira Negrouche's *The Olive Trees' Jazz* and Claire Malroux's *Daybreak*, both published in 2020, and Vénus Khoury-Ghata's *The Water People*, published in 2018.

DEEMA K. SHEHABI is a Palestinian-American poet, essayist, and editor. Deema is the author of *Thirteen Departures from the Moon* and co-editor with Beau Beausoleil of *Al-Mutanabbi Street Starts Here*, for which she received a Northern California Book Award. She's also co-author of *Diaspo/Renga* with Marilyn Hacker and winner of the Nazim Hikmet poetry competition in 2018. Deema's work has appeared in poets.org, *Los Angeles Review of Books*, *Prairie Schooner*, *The Massachusetts Review*, *Michigan Quarterly Review,* and in the anthologies *Heaven Looks Like Us* and *Ask the Night for a Dream*.

Also available from Interlink

IN JERUSALEM
AND OTHER POEMS
1997-2018
By Tamim Al-Barghouti

First English translation of celebrated Palestinian Poet

Born in 1977, Tamim Al-Barghouti is probably one of the most widely read Palestinian poets of his generation. His poetry readings are attended by thousands, sometimes packing stadiums and amphitheaters. The reception of his poetry among a diverse audience from various backgrounds and age groups is a testimony to the vitality of the centuries-old tradition of classical Arabic poetry. The poems in this collection were written in Cairo, Ramallah, Amman, Washington, DC and Berlin between 1996 and 2016. In 2007, Al-Barghouti's long poem "In Jerusalem," which describes an aborted journey to the city, became something of a street poem. Palestinian newspapers dubbed Al-Barghouti "The Poet of Jerusalem." To this day, his posters hang on the streets of Jerusalem and other Palestinian cities, where key chains are sold with his picture on them. Sections of the poem have even become ring-tones blaring out from cell phones across the Arab world, and children compete in memorizing and reciting it. "In Jerusalem" and other poems by Al-Barghouti have also had millions views on various TV Channels as well as on the internet, winning the poet an exceptional celebrity status in the Arab World. On the January 26, 2011, one day after the Egyptian Revolution that toppled President Hosni Mubarak, Al-Barghouti wrote the lyrical poem "Hanet"; its Arabic title roughly translates as "It's Close." With the internet down, he faxed the poem to a Cairo newspaper, copies of which were distributed in Tahrir Square. Soon after, Al-Jazeera TV Channel broadcast a recording of it and a video of his reading was projected in the Square every couple of hours on makeshift screens.

Also available from Interlink

I DON'T WANT THIS POEM TO END
Early and Late Poems
By Mahmoud Darwish
Translated by Mohammad Shaheen
Introduction by Elias Khoury

When the Palestinian poet Mahmoud Darwish died in 2008, his friends visited his home and retrieved poems and writings some of which are gathered together in this volume, translated into English for the first time. They include three collections from different phases in Darwish's writing career, as well as reminiscences by friends drawn from the poet's final years, and a moving account of the discovery of the new poems in this collection.

"[In] this alluring volume . . . Translator and editor Shaheen treats the poetic text as an artifact of a life in language, recognizing that Darwish's movement through language was inevitably both personal and political. The title of the collection and some of its lines 'might be said to be the last words spoken by the poet,' observes Elias Khoury in his introduction. Such graceful contextualization allows readers to appreciate the nuances of the translation and Darwish's own words: 'He says to her as they gaze at a rose, Which scratches the wall: death came a little nearer to me,' Darwish writes in the title poem. That these may have been among Darwish's last words heightens the emotional impact of both the poem's craft and the faultless translation. The image of the rose functions as an emblem for the possibility- of empathy, kindness, and enlightenment—that art opens within political life. By carefully framing Darwish's poetry as the record of a citizen inhabiting the complexities of Palestine's political landscape, Shaheen delivers a volume ideally suited to both scholars and newcomers to Darwish's body of work."
— *Publishers Weekly* (starred review)

Also available from Interlink

ALMOND BLOSSOMS & BEYOND
By Mahmoud Darwish
Translated by Mohammad Shaheen

The first English translation of recent poetry by the late Mahmoud Darwish, the most important Palestinian contemporary poet.

Almond Blossoms and Beyond is one of the last collections of poetry that Mahmoud Darwish left to the world. Composed of brief lyric poems and the magnificent sustained Exile cycle, *Almond Blossoms* holds an important place in Darwish's unparalleled oeuvre. It distills his late style, in which, though the specter of death looms and weddings turn to funerals, he threads the pulses and fragilities and beauties of life into the lines of his poems. Their liveliness is his own response to the collection's final call to bid "Farewell / Farewell, to the poetry of pain."

"I can only hope that the day will soon come, especially in English, when Darwish's night and dream, jasmine and almond blossoms are seen for what they are: the private lexicon of a singular and eternal, timeless voice in the history of human literature." — **Fady Joudah**

"*Almond Blossoms and Beyond* [. . . is] a complex counterpoint between the personal and the political, the poetic and the poetological (poetry about poetry), the reflective and the polemical, the real and the surreal. These shifts are rapid but graceful, a grace that is well captured by Shaheen's translations . . . a carefully, almost symmetrically structured collection . . . beautifully produced."— ***Electronic Intifada***

"Darwish, who died in 2008, writes lyric poems about uprootedness, exile, love, and the idea of death, which seems to throb between his lines . . . clear, simple, and yet elusive language charged with sharp visual images and vibrant musical beats . . . Darwish's transformative language delights."
— ***Library Journal***

Also available from Interlink

PALESTINE AS METAPHOR
By Mahmoud Darwish
Translated by Amira El-Zein &
Carolyn Forché

"A brilliant poet—certainly the most gifted of his generation in the Arab world." — **Edward Said**

Palestine as Metaphor consists of a series of interviews with Mahmoud Darwish, which have never appeared in English before. The interviews are a wealth of information on the poet's personal life, his relationships, his numerous works, and his tragedy. They illuminate Darwish's conception of poetry as a supreme art that transcends time and place.

Several writers and journalists conducted the interviews, including a Lebanese poet, a Syrian literary critic, three Palestinian writers, and an Israeli journalist. Each encounter took place in a different city from Nicosia to London, Paris, and Amman.

These vivid dialogues unravel the threads of a rich life haunted by the loss of Palestine and illuminate the genius and the distress of a major world poet.

"These interviews are a rich trove of his reflections on his art, personal revelations, and political insight . . . vivid and fluid translations, one clearly hears Darwish's voice: self-assured yet sensitive, witty yet sincere.
— ***New York Review of Books***

"Any reader who has enjoyed Darwish's poetry or prose collections would surely also enjoy these exchanges." — ***ArabLit***